To

Walk

In

Stardust

A Selection Of Writings For Those Who Dream

By Flavia Weedn

Roserich Designs, Ltd.
Carpinteria, California

Library of Congress Cataloging in Publication Data

TO WALK IN STARDUST
PRINTED IN USA
ISBN 0-913289-12-4

*This book is dedicated
to those of us who dream.*

*Some give up
and put their dreams away
and some pick up the pieces
and begin again.
But all of us know...
the real joy is not in the dream —
but in the dreaming.*

*...but
they
walk
in
stardust.*

◆　◆　◆

There's
a secret
place
inside
our hearts
where
all our
dreams
are born.

◆ ◆ ◆

*If we
could hold
dreams
in our hands
they would
sparkle
and shine
like stars.*

♦ ♦ ♦

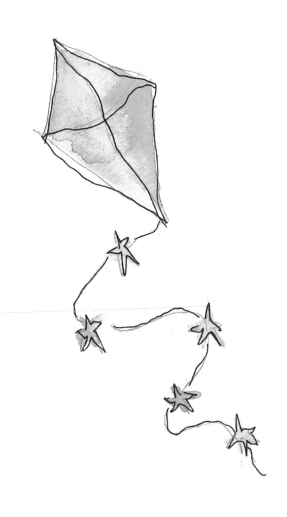

*The spirit
within you
remains
a free thing
filled
with
boundless
dreams
to share.*

◆ ◆ ◆

We are
the
silent
music
makers...

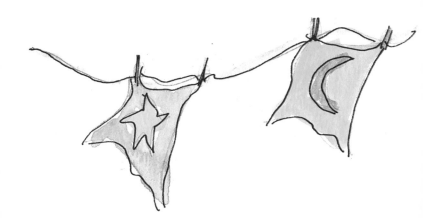

*...the
dreamers,
the
followers
of
fancy.*

♦ ♦ ♦

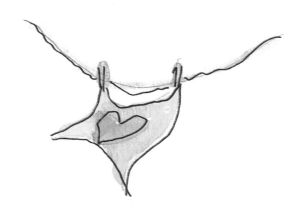

*We
are
made of
bits
of heaven
and
pieces
of
dreams.*

♦   ♦   ♦

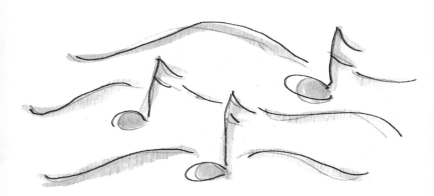

*God
gives
us
music.
We are
our
own
instruments.*

◆ ◆ ◆

*Listen
to
the
sound
of
your
own
song.*

◆   ◆   ◆

In
true
joy
there
is
splendour...

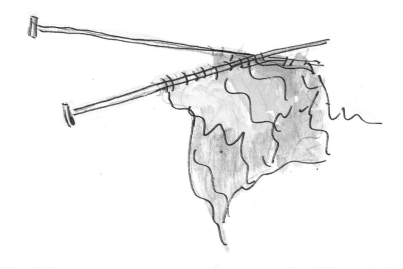

*...and
its
threads
run
through
the beginning
of every
dream.*

• • •

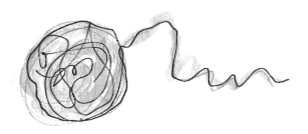

*Life is
the music
that
dances
through
our days,
our nights
and
our years.*

◆ ◆ ◆

Does
not
a city
as well
as
a song
begin
with
a dream?

◆ ◆ ◆

Dreaming
is
learning.
Know
when you
have
outgrown
a dream
and when
it is time
to move on.

◆   ◆   ◆

*When you
dance
to your
own music...*

*...your
dreams
soar
with
the wind.*

♦ ♦ ♦

*Those
who
reach
touch
the
stars.*

♦ ♦ ♦

*Life
has
no
endings,
only
beginnings.*

◆ ◆ ◆

*Within
every
ordinary
moment
there
are
millions
of
miracles.*

◆　◆　◆

*Those
who
take rides
on rainbows
and
hear music
from
dusty
violins...*

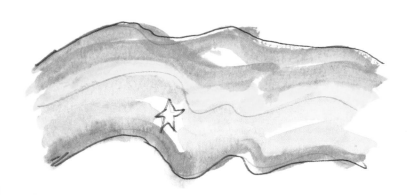

...know
that
life
is
a
many
splendoured
thing.

• • •

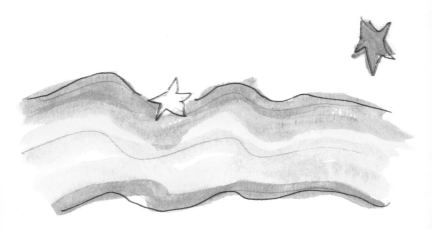

*When
you
dream...
beautiful
things
happen.*

◆ ◆ ◆

Each
of us
was born
to hear
music…

*...for
the heart
dances
each
time
it dreams.*

◆ ◆ ◆

*To
those
who
believe,
there
is
no
failure.*

◆　◆　◆

*If
days
offered
dreams
for
sale...*

*...what
would
you
buy?*

◆ ◆ ◆

This is
your time
and
you
are a part
of the
world.
Take
the risk
of living.

◆ ◆ ◆

Those
unafraid
to seek
are the
finders
of treasures.

◆ ◆ ◆

*May
your
dreams
be
touched
with
magic.*

◆ ◆ ◆

*Imagination
is
the
seed
of
dreams.*

*Nurture it
and
you will
harvest
its rewards.*

◆ ◆ ◆

Life
has
a thousand
joys,
each one
found
in the heart.

◆ ◆ ◆

To
believe
in life
is
to believe
every wish
will be
heard.

❖   ❖   ❖

*Time
is a
gypsy...
scattering
stars
and
weaving
dreams.*

◆   ◆   ◆

To
live
is
miracle
enough.

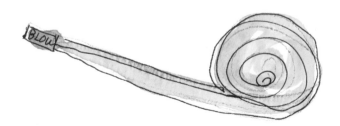

*All of
life
is filled
with
wonder
and surprises.*

♦ ♦ ♦

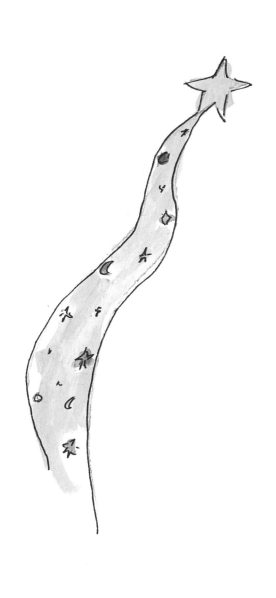

*Follow
your
star
wherever
it
takes
you.*

◆ ◆ ◆

*Dreams
riding
on wheels
of fancy
take us
to faraway
places
only
the heart
can see.*

♦ ♦ ♦

Love
all of life.
It is
the stuff
of which
dreams
are
made.

◆   ◆   ◆

*Cut not
the
wings
of
your
dreams...*

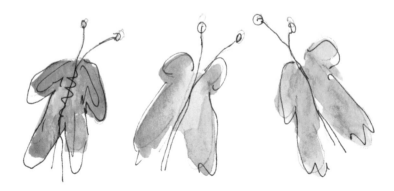

*...for
they
are the
heartbeat
and the
freedom
of your
soul.*

◆ ◆ ◆

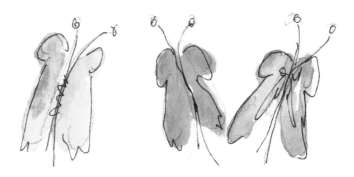

THE BOWL OF LIFE

*Into
each
heart
is born
a spirit
filled
with
wonder.*

◆　◆　◆

*When
you aim
for the stars
you can
never
stop
believing.*

◆　◆　◆

*Wonder
is the
stardust
of
our
dreams.*

❖ ❖ ❖

*Miracles
come
in all
shapes
and
sizes...*

*...and
happen
to those
who
believe
in them.*

◆ ◆ ◆

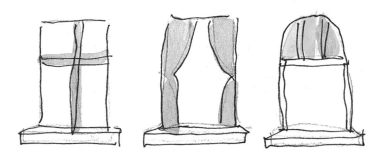

*Listen
to the
dream makers
for
they are
the
guardians
of wonder.*

♦   ♦   ♦

The End

Flavia Weedn makes her home in Santa Barbara, California with her husband Jack and a big white cat named Charlie. She enjoys her family, her work, and the simple things in life.

Flavia has been painting and writing professionally for over 25 years but her work of late is truly her finest. Being a writer as well as an illustrator puts incredible demands on her time, however the endless deadlines never seem to scatter her. Painting and writing are Flavia's private passions, and she eagerly retreats daily into her octagonal studio, vintage 1940. French windows look out upon an acre of trees and a meadow overlooking the ocean. This brings her pleasure and allows her to gather her thoughts calmly while she absorbs the brilliance of this area she has chosen for her home; her beloved Santa Barbara.

When asked what her work represents she says quietly, "The incredibility of life that I feel; the beauty I see in ordinary moments and the need for people to express themselves honestly. In short, I try to bring hope to the human spirit."

Other Flavia titles include *Wrapped In A Ribbon, Softly In Silver Sandals, Moments Shared* and *The Prize, a collection of seven vignettes.* Each are available through Roserich Designs, Ltd., PO Box 1030, Carpinteria, CA 93013-1030. Flavia is currently working on a library of collected writings.

If you wish to know more about Flavia, please write to:
The Flavia Collectors' Club, PO Box GG, Carpinteria, CA 93013-1030